Original title:

Whispers Beneath the Mistletoe

Author: Henry Beaumont

ISBN HARDBACK: 978-9916-90-966-9

ISBN PAPERBACK: 978-9916-90-967-6

Echoes of Soft Embrace

In a world of gentle hugs,
The cats are plotting bugs.
With every cuddle, they schemed,
On our snacks, they all dreamed.

Whiskers twitch as they lay,
Making mischief each day.
If you steal their sunny spot,
Prepare for battle — they won't stop!

Beneath the Twinkling Boughs

Underneath the twinkling lights,
Squirrels host their late-night flights.
Santa's sleigh? Oh, it's a ruse,
Just a ride on raccoons and moose!

Carols sung with a off-key beat,
While mice dance on tiny feet.
With every bite of cookie dough,
The Christmas tree starts to glow!

Shadows of Festive Wishes

Elves are trading wooden toys,
For secret snacks and giggling noises.
They lasso sleighs with tinsel ropes,
Imagining dreams and silly hopes.

In shadows where the cookies lie,
A quick snack break — oh my, oh my!
Frosty dance with a wobbly spin,
His carrot nose, is it made of sin?

Unseen Words in the Frost

Frosty letters on the pane,
Deciphering a frosty bane.
Snowflakes giggle, swirling bright,
They just love the winter night.

With every word that meets the chill,
Comes a snowman, quiet and still.
Mittens whisper their woolly fate,
While hot cocoa contemplates its weight!

Gentle Rain of Unspoken Affection

Drops of love fall from afar,
Puddles form where feelings are.
Umbrellas made of secret glances,
Dancing hearts in rainy chances.

Wetting sidewalks with shy dreams,
We slip and slide on laughter beams.
A storm of joy that makes us grin,
Splashing puddles, let the fun begin!

The clouds conspire with cheeky glee,
Pattering softly, just you and me.
Whispers fall like gentle rain,
Soak me through, forget the pain.

Sunshine peeks through milky skies,
As love blooms where the puddle lies.
Together we'll roam in raindrops' cheer,
In this wet world, you're my dear!

Finding Warmth in the Chill

Winter winds can be a bear,
But cozy blankets show they care.
Hot cocoa mixed with silly grins,
We laugh as snowflakes kiss our chins.

Our socks are thick, our spirits light,
In knitted wear, we look a sight!
A snowball fight, oh what a thrill,
One wrong move, we might just spill!

Fires crackle, hissing whispers,
S'mores in hand, we're true resistors.
Together we'll melt the frost away,
Chasing the cold, come what may!

So hold me tight 'neath snowy skies,
In your warmth, I find no lies.
With you, the chill is a laughing friend,
Our winter antics never end!

Silent Blessings of the Season

Leaves fall down in vibrant hues,
They dress the ground like fancy shoes.
With pumpkins wink and apples grin,
We dance with spices on our skin.

Hats and scarves emerge with flair,
As laughter fills the crisp, cool air.
Each smile is a tiny blessing,
In this joyful, wild dressing.

Cider swirls in autumn's hand,
As friends recount the summer's land.
With every bite of pumpkin pie,
A giggle bursts; oh me, oh my!

So gather 'round in warmth and cheer,
With silent blessings, we hold dear.
The season wraps our hearts in gold,
A funny tale that's always told!

Soft Serenades in the Midnight Chill

In winter's grip, we snuggle tight,
Our breath like steam, a frosty sight.
You steal the covers, but that's okay,
I'll just cuddle closer, hip hooray!

The cats are plotting, yes they're scheming,
On icy nights, they think of dreaming.
They pounce on toes, oh what a fright,
Soft serenades in the bold moonlight.

Hot cocoa spills, a marshmallow dive,
Sipping slowly, we try to survive.
Laughter echoes in this snowy hall,
As snowflakes outside begin to fall.

So grab your blanket, don't be shy,
With my warm hugs, let the chill fly by.
We'll hum sweet tunes through the frosty air,
Soft serenades, our own night fair!

Tales of Love in the Silent Night

Under the stars, our whispers play,
Sharing secrets in a silly way.
You say I'm cute, with a cheeky grin,
As I trip on ice, oh boy, take care in!

Your heart's a snowman, fluffy and round,
But your dance moves? They don't make a sound.
We laugh through the night like a couple of fools,
In our winter wonderland, where laughter rules.

With each little hug, the world melts away,
You steal a kiss, what do I say?
My cheeks are chilly, but your love's a fire,
In this silent night, hearts never tire.

So let's tell tales that twinkle and shine,
Under the moonlight, with hands intertwined.
In snowdrifts of laughter, we'll find our way,
Tales of love that will never decay.

Secrets Held by the Icy Veil

The world outside is dressed in white,
While we hide secrets in the night.
A snowball here, a cheeky surprise,
You sneak up on me, with mischief in your eyes.

Ice skates squeak as we glide in a rush,
I pretend to be cool, but I stumble and blush.
You laugh so hard, your cheeks turn red,
A perfect moment, that's easily said.

Under the stars, with snowflakes afloat,
You whisper sweet nothings while making a snow coat.
In the icy veil, our laughter's a spark,
Every secret we share lights up the dark.

So let's build a snow fort, with pillows galore,
And crown ourselves kings of this winter lore.
With giggles and warmth, we'll set sail on this spree,
Secrets wrapped tight, just you and me.

The Unseen Dance of Winter Hearts

Two hearts collide in the frosty breeze,
Chasing snowflakes, enjoying the freeze.
Your mittened hand slips right into mine,
We stumble around, yelling, "Oh, that's divine!"

The snowman frowns with his carrot nose,
For we made him dance in our winter clothes.
He thinks he's serious, but what does he know?
We waltz right past, with a flurry of snow.

Under the twinkling of streetlight stars,
We run like children, dodging snow cars.
Laughter and joy in each icy breath,
In this unseen dance, there's no sense of depth.

So here's to the winter, both bold and bright,
With caps and gloves, we'll dance through the night.
For in every leap, every frosty part,
Lies the unseen dance of our winter hearts.

Quiet Promises in the Midwinter Gleam

Snowflakes dance like they're on a spree,
Whispers of promises, just wait and see.
The mugs of cocoa start to cheer,
While squirrels plot their heist, oh dear!

Fuzzy socks are partners in this crime,
Lazily lounging, it's the best time.
Wrapped in blankets, we laugh and snore,
Dreaming of cookies, who could want more?

Intimate Whispers of Twinkling Lights

The lights twinkle like a cheeky grin,
Spreading warmth from the house within.
They giggle softly, "We're not so bright,
But who's counting? We're a pretty sight!"

A cat chases shadows in the glow,
Declaring war on all things below.
With ornaments tangled, a festive mess,
Even the tree knows how to impress!

Love Notes Carried on the Winter Breeze

Winter's breeze sings a chilly tune,
Love notes flurry around like a cartoon.
With cheeks rosy and laughter galore,
Hot chocolate spills as we tumble to the floor!

The snowman winks with a frosty shake,
"What's better than love? A good piece of cake!"
We giggle and munch as the snowflakes fall,
Making sweet memories, oh what a ball!

Rumors of Romance in the Frosted Air

Frosted windows hide secret schemes,
While snowflakes whisper about wild dreams.
"Do they like pie?" the icicles tease,
Or is it hot cocoa that brings them to their knees?

In the frosted air, laughter is bold,
Each flurry of love, a story unfold.
With mittens mismatched, we dance and we twirl,
In this winter wonderland, let's give it a whirl!

Hidden Embrace 'Neath the Starlit Sky

Under the sky, so vast and wide,
I tripped on a rock, feeling the tide.
Stars were laughing in their twinkling way,
While I fumbled for words I couldn't say.

A squirrel peeked in, with eyes like a thief,
Stealing my thoughts, beyond belief.
With every giggle from the cosmic spree,
I wondered if the stars were laughing at me.

The moon winked down with a silvery grin,
I waved back awkwardly, feeling the spin.
In this sneaky dance of shadows and light,
I lost my balance but found pure delight.

Hidden embraces of laughter and sighs,
Beneath the starlit theatre, truths never lie.
With every bump and joyful mistake,
Under the stars, our hearts would awake.

Unspoken Bonds Amidst the Icicles

Icicles dangle like hair on a cat,
While I scale the roof, looking quite flat.
Winter's chill gives us reasons to slide,
And hot cocoa dreams, with marshmallows wide.

My brother made snowman, gave him a hat,
But forgot to ensure he was sturdy and sat.
Down he went, with a splat on the snow,
Laughing, we squealed, 'It's a winter show!'

We built a fort, made of frosty delight,
In a battle of snowballs, we took to flight.
But with each throw, a slip here and there,
Our laughter echoed through the icy air.

Unspoken bonds formed in chilly embrace,
With winter's mischief coursing through space.
Each slip and slide is a tale to retell,
In the heart of the cold, we find warmth as well.

Heartfelt Secrets in the Candlelit Glow

Candles flicker with secrets they keep,
In the kitchen, where whispered thoughts creep.
Mom's baking cookies, oh what a delight,
But who's stealing dough in the soft candlelight?

A glimmer of chocolate, a sprinkle of fun,
We're crafting our smiles, one by one.
But sugar's a trickster, we end up in giggles,
As flour explodes, and the dough softly wiggles.

"Shh," I say, as the batter takes flight,
But laughter's too loud in the soft, warm night.
With frosting on noses and cheeky grins wide,
Heartfelt secrets are shared, side by side.

In this cozy glow, where dreams intertwine,
Every little mischief feels oh-so divine.
Our hearts are as sweet as the treats that we bake,
In the dance of the evening, all memories awake.

Enchanted Moments in the Winter Garden

Snowflakes twirl like dancers on air,
In the garden, where magic hangs fair.
We chase winter sprites through the frosty leaf,
With giggles and joy, we're the kings of belief.

The garden gnomes grumble, caught in the prank,
While we strategic snowball, right by the tank.
Each throw a surprise, laughter takes flight,
As snow drifts appear in the soft winter night.

A penguin appeared! Oh wait, that's my cat,
Dressed in a sweater, how silly is that?
With every new moment, enchantment unfolds,
While the world wears its white, we're brave and bold.

In this winter wonder, where fun comes alive,
The garden is magic, where giggles survive.
Let's dance with the snowflakes, in joy take our stand,
Enchanted forever, in this playful land.

Soft Breezes Through Frosted Pines

Soft breezes kiss the frosted trees,
Whispering jokes with playful ease.
Pines chuckle as they sway and creak,
'They really need to work on their peak!'

As snowflakes fall in fluffy heaps,
The squirrels plot for winter's sleeps.
'Time to gather nuts and snacks galore,
I think we'll need a bigger store!'

A bird appears with a comical tweet,
'Winter fashion? It's so offbeat!'
His feathers puffed like a popcorn ball,
'At least I'm warm; that's the main call!'

Through frosted pines, the giggles flow,
A comedy show, nature's own show.
With frozen smiles and twinkling eyes,
Winter's humor, the best surprise!

Gentle Declarations of Affection

Roses are red, violets are blue,
If you were a car, I'd steal you too.
But please don't blush, let's keep it light,
I swear it's love at first sight!

Your laughter is music, sweet and clear,
Like cats in a box, I'm drawn near.
With quirky quirks and silly charms,
You've stolen my heart, without alarms!

A dinner for two? It's all on me;
I'll even cook, you'll be so free.
Just promise not to run away,
If I burn the toast on this fine day!

So let's dance through life without a care,
With goofy grins, how can we bear?
Holding hands in a silly stance,
Consider this my grand romance!

Secrets of the Glowing Hearth

By the glowing hearth, secrets we share,
Like why my socks just never pair.
'They vanish,' I gasp with wide-eyed glee,
'Heading to Mars, for a sock jubilee!'

The flames crackle and pop in delight,
As we laugh at the shadows that dance in the night.
A marshmallow conspiracy is underway,
Sticky fingers, oh what a fun play!

There's life in the logs, or so they say,
Each one a story, each splinter, a way.
'If only these embers could tell us more,'
'Of love, of loss, and snacks to explore!'

So gather 'round, let's spin a yarn,
With warmth from the fire that brings no harm.
In the hearth's embrace, let laughter ignite,
For secrets unfold under the starry night!

The Language of Falling Snow

Falling snow, a silent parade,
Making whispers in frosty shade.
Each snowflake giggles, takes its flight,
Landing on noses, what a silly sight!

They shimmy and twist in a frosty waltz,
While I trip on my boots, oh what faults!
Snowmen are sculpted with carrots and flair,
But one keeps melting; it's just not fair!

Even the trees wear winter's lace,
As snowflakes dance at a merry pace.
They gather and meet in heaps and glows,
'This is our time; see how it flows!'

So let's embrace this snowy blend,
With snowball fights that never end.
In laughter and joy, we learn anew,
The language of snow: so funny, so true!

Unheard Melodies of Winter

The snowflakes dance, a waltz so fine,
I trip on ice, a clumsy line.
The frost sings tunes of chilly glee,
While squirrels mock me from a tree.

My nose is red, like Rudolph's flair,
My coat's so puffy, I float in air.
The winter's grip, a frosty hug,
Yet here I am, just a frozen bug.

Hot cocoa spills, a chocolate sea,
I frown at spillage—neglecting me.
But laughter rings with every slip,
In winter's grip, it's joy I sip.

So tread with care on pathways white,
Where every slide is pure delight.
Unheard melodies drift and twirl,
In a winter wonderland, I whirl.

Love Notes in the Icicle's Edge

An icicle hangs like Cupid's dart,
Suspenseful love, a frosty art.
It drips with hope, a chilly kiss,
Yet I fear slips could ruin this.

You wrote me notes in frosty air,
But scribbled lines lead to despair.
For every heart with melting might,
A slippery path turned into fright.

We take our chances on this ledge,
With hearts of warmth by icy edge.
Oh love, my dear, let's just embrace,
And pray we don't fall—what a chase!

So let's face the freeze, hand in hand,
While dodging icicles—oh, so grand!
These love notes hang with frozen cheer,
In winter's chill, you're all I hear.

Reveries in the Quiet Snowfall

In quiet snow, time seems to freeze,
A blissful pause, a gentle breeze.
I build a snowman, a goofy chap,
With button eyes and a woolly gap.

The flakes come down, a blanket white,
I grab my sled—it's pure delight!
But on the way, I tumble 'round,
Snow angels made without a sound.

The world's aglow, a hushed affair,
A winter dream, beyond compare.
I sip my tea, all snug and warm,
While snowflakes cradle my heart in charm.

So here I sit, in blissful thought,
With memories of fun, I've gladly caught.
These reveries, in snowflakes' call,
Remind me softly—the best is all.

The Silent Bond of Shared Moments

With you, I share a snowball fight,
We launch our laughs in pure delight.
But who knew a throw could miss,
And end up with a snowy kiss?

We sip hot soup, a bowl for two,
Your slurpy charm just cracks me, too.
In every chuckle, a bond so warm,
In winter's chill, it's pure love's charm.

The chilly nights are wrapped in gold,
With stories shared, we bravely hold.
We stroll past trees with lights aglow,
In quiet moments, our spirits flow.

So let's embrace this frosty spree,
With giggles and warmth, just you and me.
In winter's grasp, our hearts align,
In shared moments, love's spark will shine.

Flurries of Unsaid Words

In a world where thoughts take flight,
My cat steals my food with delight.
Every missed chance, a snowflake flees,
While I debate, 'Should I sneeze?'

The neighbor's dog barks, such a thrill,
While I trip over my own quill.
Words freeze in my mouth like winter's chill,
But my laugh echoes louder still.

I ponder life's big cosmic joke,
As I search for a pen and choke.
Each giggle unsaid dances in the air,
Yet I'm stuck counting socks to declare.

So here's to the lines I never write,
Like fairy lights that flicker at night.
They swirl and twirl in winter's embrace,
As I sip hot cocoa, life's gentle pace.

Dreams Wrapped in Holiday Joy

This year I dreamed of cookies galore,
But ended up face first on the floor.
My holiday plans fell flat as a pie,
While my aunt nearly set herself on fire.

Wrapping gifts so tightly with a grin,
I discovered I'd wrapped my own chin.
Each bow and ribbon a puzzling plight,
Who knew 'tis the season for wrapping tracks tight?

The eggnog cheers turn to splutters and laughs,
As uncle Joe tells his thirty wrong paths.
Each tale a delight, though they've all gone stale,
With every sip, we plot a new trail.

So cheers to mishaps that make our hearts bright,
To holidays filled with pure silly sight.
We'll chortle and giggle, our spirits will soar,
In dreams wrapped in joy, forever explore.

Unspoken Stories of the Season

The Christmas lights twinkle with festive flair,
But half of them flash like a small scare.
I strung them up willing them to glow,
Only to find out they dance like a show.

The turkey's singing, or so it seems,
As I struggle to fulfill the grand dreams.
Each bite of stuffing is a miracle made,
Yet half of it's burnt – call it a charade.

With family gathered and stories so bold,
Grandpa, with his tales, is the funniest told.
Each laugh and chuckle becomes pure gold,
Even if half of them are already old.

So here's to the stories we've yet to share,
To the memories made while we try to prepare.
In the season of whimsy, we'll keep it aglow,
With unspoken adventures waiting to flow.

Enigmas in the Frosted Air

The snowflakes whisper secrets untold,
As I fumble my mittens, feeling quite bold.
Each flake falls softly, a riddle so nice,
I wonder why my nose is a block of ice.

When winter arrives, my hair frizzes wide,
Like a bird's nest that's taken a ride.
Each gust of wind offers mystery deep,
As I trip over boots, into a snowdrift I leap.

The frost on the window plays peek-a-boo,
What stories they hold, if they only knew.
My thoughts float away, like kites in the sky,
While I ponder the meaning of 'why oh why'?

So here's to the enigmas that frostbitten days bring,
To laughter and joy, let's hear the bells ring!
In the chill of the air, let our humor take flight,
As we navigate life, bundled up tight!

Treasures Wrapped in Quietude

In the stillness, socks disappear,
They dance around without a cheer.
Left one sings, right one contends,
Lost in laundry, where time bends.

The cat now rules the cozy couch,
Waging war with a plastic pouch.
Sighs of silence, oh what a hoot,
Finding treasures in every boot!

Coffee brewed, spills on the floor,
It's a masterpiece, nothing more.
Quietude holds the greatest jest,
Amidst the mess, we find our best.

Tick-tock clocks on a lazy spree,
In this calm, we'll let it be.
Laughter echoes, joy and glee,
Wrapped in quiet, just you and me.

Ballet of Hearts in the Twilight

Under the moon, stars twirl and spin,
My heart's a dancer, where to begin?
With two left feet, I stumble and fall,
The twilight stage, I give my all!

The crickets cheer in their nightly croak,
As I moonwalk on a piece of oak.
Spinning round with total flair,
Lost in the moment, without a care.

Butterflies giggle, they take their seats,
While fireflies shine with blinking beats.
In this ballet, all's quite absurd,
Dancing with silliness, not a word!

As night wraps up, the show ends sweet,
With laughter echoing, a funny repeat.
In the twilight, our hearts take flight,
Together in dance, what a sight!

Covert Hope in the Candlelight

In the candle's flicker, dreams ignite,
Hiding beneath the surreal light.
Whispers of hope, they softly sway,
In shadows play, they find their way.

Dreams sneak out in the darkest hour,
With a twinkle, they bloom like a flower.
A mouse taps out a rhythmic tune,
As the cat snoozes under the moon.

Jars of jam line up like soldiers,
In night's army, the midnight holders.
Creating plans for tomorrow's feast,
While silent giggles won't be ceased.

Hope's a sneak thief, in joy it thrives,
Wrapped in secrets, where laughter derives.
By candlelight, we plot and plan,
Covert desires in a dreamland span.

Unveiling Joys of the Solstice

The solstice comes, the sun plays nice,
Day's so long, it must think twice.
In celebration, we sip and share,
With sun-kissed skins and messy hair.

Picnics bloom like daisies wild,
Where sandwiches lie 'neath a giggling child.
Ants join in the feast without shame,
Gathering crumbs, they join the game.

Fireflies blink, a grand parade,
In summer's warmth, the worries fade.
Hula-hoops whirl, laughter ignites,
As evening's glow turns into delights.

With every sunset's soft embrace,
We find the joy in the crowded space.
Unveiling treasures, each little cheer,
In solstice's heart, summer is here!

Echoed Laughter in Winter's Embrace

In winter's chill, we all come alive,
With snowball fights that make us thrive.
Hot cocoa spills on our favorite sweaters,
We laugh so hard, let's make it better!

Footprints trudge through the snowy ground,
Chasing laughter, joy is found.
A penguin slide, oh what a sight,
The neighbors whisper, 'What a night!'

Frosty noses, cheeks brightly red,
Each joke shared warms hearts instead.
In the glow of lights, we play and tease,
Winter's joy is such a breeze!

So gather 'round, let the laughter ring,
For in the cold, our hearts take wing.
With every chuckle, every cheer,
Winter's magic is crystal clear!

The Fabric of Togetherness

Stitching moments in a patchwork way,
Each thread a memory, bright as day.
Sewing laughter into every seam,
Togetherness, life's greatest dream.

A mismatched quilt of silly tales,
Where humor flows like wind in gales.
Themes of chaos, love, and cheer,
We wear our stories year by year.

Crafting joy with hearts aglow,
Baking cookies as kids run to and fro.
We spin and twirl in this fun parade,
In every stitch, our bond is made.

So let's gather close, share our thread,
With laughter as the passion we spread.
For life's fabric, vibrant and bright,
Is woven tight with love and light!

Dreaming under the Winter Stars

Under a blanket of sparkly white,
We dream together under the night.
Snowflakes twinkle like stars on cue,
And winter whispers, 'I love you!'

With each frosty breath, we gaze in awe,
At constellations that never draw law.
A snowman nearby wearing a hat,
Looks like he's ready to join our chat!

The moon grins wide with a silvery glow,
While we share secrets only snowmen know.
Giggles erupt with each chilly breeze,
As our dreams dance like leaves on trees.

So let's count the stars, one by one,
In this frosty realm, we have so much fun.
Hand in hand, with hearts aglow,
Under winter stars, together we flow!

Illusions Unraveled in the Cold

In the freezing air, our breath does steam,
Our noses redder than a ripe tangerine.
Slipping on ice, oh what a sight!
Down we go, laughter takes flight!

The mirage of snow, so perfectly white,
Until you realize, it's really quite light.
'Tis just a trick, it's slippery fun,
Like chasing a cat, we'll never outrun!

Snowmen melting with grins so wide,
In this winter wonder, we take it in stride.
The illusion of warmth in the coldest of days,
Turns frowns to laughter in giggling plays!

So let's embrace winter, with joyous delight,
We'll conquer the chill, hearts shining bright.
For in this madness, laughter prevails,
Through illusions of winter, our joy never fails!

Underneath the Evergreen Canopy

Beneath the trees so tall and grand,
I found a squirrel with a nut in hand.
He winked at me, with great delight,
And promptly dropped it, oh what a sight!

The pinecone fell and knocked his hat,
He cursed the wind and gave a spat.
A dance for joy, he did perform,
While I just laughed, safe from the storm.

The owls hooted at my silly laughs,
As I started counting their feathery crafts.
"Who's there?" they asked with a gaze so wise,
"Just nature's stand-up, under these skies!"

With every chuckle, the woodland smiled,
Even the trees seemed more beguiled.
So here beneath this leafy dome,
We share a giggle, nature's home.

Embraces Frozen in Time

In winter's grasp, the snowflakes twirl,
I slipped and slid, in a dizzy whirl.
My dog laughed hard, as I took a dive,
He wagged his tail, said, "You're quite alive!"

The snowman stared with his carrot nose,
I told him secrets, my frozen woes.
He chuckled back, in a frosty tone,
"Just keep it cool, don't melt your own!"

Hot cocoa dances in my chilly hands,
Marshmallows float, by my snowy plans.
Each sip a hug, each swirl a dream,
But add some rum? Oh, what a scheme!

Time freezes fast, as laughter lifts,
In sledding rumbles, and snowball GIFs.
So here's to winter, laugh and play,
Embraced by chill, we seize the day!

Ties that Bind in the Cold

Wrapped in coats, as thick as a bear,
We brave the cold, without a care.
Hot tea warms us from head to toe,
But outside, the winds still fiercely blow!

We built a fort, with walls of snow,
A cozy nook where friendships grow.
From frozen toes to frosty cheeks,
We share our tales, as laughter peaks.

Outside a dog, with a coat so bright,
Joined our fun, in pure delight.
He rolled and tumbled, a furry clown,
As we all laughed, forgetting frowns.

Together in chill, we find our cheer,
These ties that bind, make winter dear.
So grab your friends, and let's all meet,
In frozen bliss, where hearts don't freeze!

Subdued Serenades in Flickering Light

By candlelight, the shadows dance,
A mouse peeks in for a quick glance.
He tiptoes past without a care,
While I scribble rhymes in my cozy chair.

The clock ticks softly, a muffled beat,
While I sip soup, a warm little treat.
"Is this poetry?" the cat does ask,
As she yawns wide, in her lazy bask.

I hum a tune, with notes so low,
The flickering flames put on a show.
And though it's quiet, the laughter's near,
In these gentle moments, love feels clear.

So in this light, where giggles sway,
I'll keep on writing, come what may.
With heart and humor, we twirl and spin,
In subdued serenades, the joy begins!

Affection's Music in the Silent Wood

In the woods where sunbeams play,
Squirrels dance in a cheeky way.
Trees gossip with the breeze so light,
While lovers swoon, but with a fright.

A deer checks its phone, oh what a sight,
Texting friends about last night's fight.
Birds chirp tunes that sound like a show,
But really just want to steal your glow.

Romance blooms in a critter's nest,
Yet all we want is just a rest.
Frogs croak love songs, but they don't rhyme,
Maybe it's nature who needs some time!

So here's to love in the leafy wood,
With conversations misunderstood.
Find a heart where the squirrels all play,
And laugh your worries gently away.

Conversations in the Frosted Air

In winter's breath, we bundle tight,
Conversations crackle, oh what a sight.
Snowflakes tumble, they ups and downs,
As we tell jokes till laughter drowns.

Gloves get lost in the frosty breeze,
We stumble and giggle like clumsy bees.
Every word drips like icicles free,
While hot cocoa warms our jubilee.

The trees wear coats of sparkling white,
While our voices dance under stars so bright.
Freezy chants make us lose our way,
But who needs a path when we're here to play?

As snowmen eavesdrop, their eyes are wide,
While kids throw snowballs, join the ride.
In this chilly chat, hearts stay warm,
We laugh through winter's magical charm.

Love's Hidden Murmur in the Holiday Glow

Under twinkling lights, love's whispers start,
With tangled lights, we trip, no art.
Cookies burn while the carols play,
Still, we smile, in the holiday fray.

Ornaments bobble, one falls with a crash,
We giggle and snort in a joyful splash.
Mistletoe hangs, a faux pas delight,
As awkward kisses take flight at night.

In the glow of warmth, our hearts get full,
While Uncle Joe's jokes are slightly dull.
Yet laughter wraps us like a snug scarf,
In this jolly mess, we find our path.

So here's to love wrapped in tinsel bright,
With every mishap, we shine more bright.
As the season spins us round and round,
In holiday cheer, true love is found.

The Quiet Magic of a December Evening

December calls with a gentle chill,
Snowflakes murmur, oh what a thrill.
We sip hot tea, let the steam arise,
While watching the stars put on their disguise.

Candles flicker in a cozy nook,
Stories unfold just like a book.
Each laugh is a gift as time draws near,
While we warm up with winter cheer.

Frosty windows make us peep and peek,
Inside our hearts, no need to speak.
The night is still, yet filled with mirth,
In every glance, we find our worth.

So come embrace this magic night,
With soft giggles and gentle light.
Let's savor the silence, feel the grace,
In December's arms, we find our place.

The Quiet Promise of December

The snowflakes dance, they twist and glide,
A winter's tale, where secrets hide.
Hot cocoa waits, all frothy and sweet,
While squirrels plot their winter feats.

The moon peeks out, a cheeky grin,
As carolers practice, where to begin.
Each door adorned with wreaths and cheer,
While cats in snooze, conquer once more, dear.

The days grow short, so dark the night,
But twinkling lights bring sheer delight.
Under blankets, we huddle so tight,
Sharing stories till morning's light.

So raise a glass to frosty fun,
For December's magic has just begun.
With laughter and love, we celebrate,
In this chilly month, oh, it's just great!

Veiled Conversations Among the Leaves

The leaves gossip in the cool, crisp air,
Whispering secrets everywhere.
They shake and rattle, their tales to weave,
As squirrels listen, they never leave.

Sunlight dapples, a patchwork quilt,
While trees debate the leaves they've built.
Some boast of colors, the reds and golds,
While others hide stories that never get told.

Wind chimes giggle, a jolly crew,
As branches sway, they join the brew.
Nature's chat shows no white lies,
As feathers flutter, beneath clear skies.

With laughter shared, and off they go,
As leaves drift down, putting on a show.
In earthy tones, their secrets stay,
In veiled conversations, they dance all day.

Heartfelt Notes on Holiday Breeze

The holiday breeze sings sweet and low,
With scents of cookies beginning to flow.
Kids write notes for Santa to see,
While dreams of toys float joyfully free.

Mittens lost and scarves askew,
As laughter erupts from each family stew.
Gift wrap battles leave quite a mess,
As puppy-dog eyes await their caress.

The fireplace crackles, oh what a sight,
As families gather, hearts feels so light.
With tales by the fire, and eggnog so grand,
The warmth of the season brings joy unplanned.

So raise your glass to the festive cheer,
As we spread love and good vibes near.
In heartfelt notes, we find our place,
Embracing the joy, in this blissful space.

Mysterious Graces of the Season

The frost paints art on windows wide,
As whispers of winter take us for a ride.
With every snowflake, a story's spun,
In the chill of the night when day is done.

Mittens dance on eager hands,
As magic weaves through frosty strands.
Ghostly shadows peek through the trees,
As we ponder the mysteries, oh, if you please!

The moonlight casts its shimmering gleam,
While everyone dreams their warmest dream.
Underneath stars, we laugh and sigh,
In mysterious graces, we learn to fly.

So gather 'round and heed the call,
Embrace the revelry, let love enthrall.
For in this season, we boldly tread,
With joyous laughter, never misled!

The Space Between Kind Words

In the midst of chatter, we often forget,
That silence can spark a good-hearted bet.
A wink, a smile, all can be heard,
Even when we fumble our own little word.

A compliment tossed like a paper plane,
Can make someone chuckle, or drive 'em insane.
With kindness on standby, you never know,
When laughter erupts, like a surprise water show.

So send out your kindness, let it take flight,
It might land on someone who truly needs light.
The space between words, a treasure indeed,
Can fill up your day like a sweet honey seed.

Whispers of kindness floating around,
Are the greatest of treasures that can be found.
So make sure to share, don't keep it all locked,
For laughter and joy bloom the best when they're stocked.

Traces of Love Under the Stars

Under the stars, where wishes collide,
Love's kindest traces can't be denied.
A giggle, a wink, oh what a sight,
Even asteroids grin at the moonlight.

We flirt with the cosmos, it's quite the affair,
While sipping space juice in our zero-grav chair.
Cupid's up there with a quirk in his bow,
Shooting hearts fully stocked, they put on a show.

With constellations dancing, we laugh and we sigh,
While aliens ponder, "Why are they so high?"
A comet zips by, sparkles fill the sky,
As we twirl in the stardust, our hearts fly high.

So here's to the nights of love's playful glance,
Under the stars, let's give joy a chance.
When traces of love wink from afar,
Embrace the madness, and reach for that star!

Embracing the Stillness

In the stillness of night, where crickets sing,
We ponder on life and its curious thing.
Like cats on a windowsill basking in rays,
We drift on our thoughts, lost in a daze.

The pause that enchants in a world full of noise,
Can turn into laughter, it can also bring poise.
Like socks in a dryer, our thoughts intertwine,
In the calmness, we find our own strange design.

Like pie on a windowsill tempting the fox,
We relish each moment, in flip-flops or crocs.
Embracing the stillness, we dance to our tune,
As the moonlight winks playfully at noon.

So next time you find that stillness feels dear,
Put on your best socks and give a loud cheer.
With laughter and joy, let calmness take hold,
In the quiet of night, let your stories unfold.

The Unveiling of Tender Yearnings

In the heart of a burger joint, love roams free,
With fries as the sidekick, come sit next to me.
Tender yearnings float like ketchup on fries,
Spilling out secrets under wide-open skies.

With hearts full of giggles and laughter so bright,
We unveil our wishes, not hiding from sight.
"Got any napkins for all of this goo?"
"Love's messy, but baby, it's tasty, it's true!"

In the world of our dreams, with milkshakes and cheers,
We sip on the wishes, conquer all fears.
With every last sprinkle, our hearts come alive,
In the sweetest of moments, we both will survive.

So let's embrace cravings, no shame in our game,
With tender yearnings sparking a flame.
For love can be funny, like fries with a dip,
In the unveiling of wishes, we take the sweet trip!

Choreography of Shadows and Frost

The shadows dance, so sly and spry,
Gliding on ice as they pass by.
Frosty feet slip and slide on cue,
Even the moon laughs, 'What a view!'

They twirl and flip on the frozen lake,
With each misstep, a giggly quake.
Snowflakes fall like frozen confetti,
As the squirrels join in, looking quite petty.

The trees clap their branches, it's quite the show,
A choreography only the cold could know.
With a bow and a cheer, they take their leave,
The shadows retreat, the winter reprieve.

And as dawn breaks, they pack up their gear,
Leaving behind a frosty veneer.
While we watch with a warm cup in hand,
I secretly wish I'd joined the band.

Furtive Meetings in the Starlit Quiet

In the garden where whispers sway,
Bunnies plot a daring getaway.
With twitching noses and ears that perk,
They meet up to scheme, oh what a perk!

Under the moon's watchful gaze,
They swap their tales of nightly maze.
Fat cats slink past, trying to sneak,
But the bunnies giggle, not a sound to leak.

The fireflies flicker, a light show near,
As secretive giggles fill the atmosphere.
With each twinkle, a plan takes flight,
For a midnight feast, oh what a sight!

As dawn approaches, they scurry away,
The starlit quiet fades with the day.
But in their hearts, the mischief stays,
Ready for another night's playful haze.

Silent Hugs of Winter

Winter wraps the world so tight,
With icy arms, a frosty sight.
The trees shiver, yet bundle and glow,
In the soft embrace of the winter snow.

Snowmen stand with carrot noses,
Waving cheerfully as each one dozes.
They dream of spring, their sunny reprieve,
But for now, they dance on winter's weave.

Hot cocoa waits by the crackling fire,
While everyone hums in cozy attire.
With marshmallow hugs floating on top,
In this chilly bliss, we never want to stop.

The cold may bite, but together we cheer,
Silent hugs of winter, they're perfectly clear.
So gather close, let the warmth unfold,
In our hearts, let the winter stories be told.

Secrets of the Holiday Glow

In the attic lies a treasure we find,
Old ornaments that spark memories combined.
With a twinkle and shimmer, they softly greet,
Whispering secrets of holidays sweet.

Laughter echoes from years gone by,
As we hang them up, oh my, oh my!
The glow lights the faces with joy anew,
A twinkling reminder of love that's true.

Cookie crumbs fall from giggling hands,
As we sneak in to steal some from pans.
Frosted snowflakes land on our nose,
Caught in a moment that forever flows.

The glow of the season, it warms our heart,
A spectrum of cheer, a beautiful art.
With each flicker of light, we dance, we sway,
In the secrets of holiday glow, we play.

Murmurs Lurking in the Chill

In winter's grasp, snowflakes skitter,
A squirrel steals a snack, oh the critter!
Frosty breath whispers, 'Don't you shiver?'
While penguins in bow ties dance, oh what a quiver!

Chattering teeth join the winter crew,
As I hail a snowman, dressed in blue.
He waves with a carrot; oh, what a view!
I swear my hat just winked—how rude of you!

Icicles hang like daggers, so nice,
I can't help but wonder, will I pay the price?
My nose is freezing, but I roll the dice,
To catch that hot cocoa—ah, it'll suffice!

As snowmen plot a fashion coup,
Wishing for sunglasses and a hot air balloon.
Beneath the chilly stars, I croon,
In winter's realm, laughter wakes too soon!

Beneath the Branches of Serendipity

Under the oak, I found a shoe,
Claiming it must belong to a kangaroo.
Flip-flops at winter? Oh, what a view!
Nature's fashion sense—oh, who knew!

Birds in tuxedos strut with flair,
While squirrels argue, 'Is this nuts fair?'
A hedgehog joins, with a prickly air,
In this wild conclave, we all share a chair.

Beneath the stars, there's a disco ball,
Rabbits breakdance, giving it their all.
A mouse DJ spins, we're having a ball,
In the forest's rave, I hear nature's call.

As twilight settles with a wink and a twirl,
I trip on mushrooms—oh, what a swirl!
Laughter erupts; it's quite the whirl,
Beneath the branches, joy starts to unfurl!

Soft Confessions in Winter's Embrace

In winter's tight hug, secrets begin,
A snowman admits, 'I'm losing my grin!'
With frosty eyebrows, he whispers, 'Let's spin,'
While snowflakes giggle at their swirling kin.

I met a penguin, who loves to rhyme,
He says his belly is always prime time.
With waddly steps, he's got style sublime,
Winter's laughter echoes, a snowball chime.

Furry friends gather under moon's glow,
They plot little plays, oh, how they steal the show!
A raccoon prances, putting on a toe,
In the winter's embrace, let the fun overflow!

So come join the laughter, the frosty delights,
As the night wears on, with magical sights.
Even penguins know how to reach great heights,
In winter's soft confessions, let's dance through the nights!

Shadows of Affection in the Glistening Night

In shadows cast by the moon's gentle light,
Lovers whisper secrets; oh, what a sight!
With cocoa warm, they huddle up tight,
While owls roll their eyes, 'Get a room, alright!'

The stars join in, playing peekaboo,
As fireflies twinkle, a sparkly view.
A chatty raccoon interrupts their hullabaloo,
Says, 'Can I join in? I've got jokes for you!'

Through the trees, whispers spread like a breeze,
Squirrels roll by, happily chattering tees.
With hearts aglow, they'll do as they please,
In the night of affection, joy is the keys.

So dance with the shadows, let laughter ignite,
In this glistening night, love feels just right.
With friends all around, and spirits in flight,
We twirl through the darkness, oh, what a delight!

Frosted Dreams in the Stillness

Snowflakes dance like tiny chefs,
Whipping up a frosty mess.
Gingerbread men with sugar coats,
Skiing on marshmallow boats.

Sipping cocoa on the run,
Running into a snowman fun.
He gave me a carrot just to eat,
Said, 'You're the one who's truly sweet!'

Penguins sledding, what a sight,
Wearing hats, oh, what delight!
Frosted dreams in chilly air,
Slipping, laughing, everywhere!

As the stars begin to gleam,
I daydream of a whipped cream dream.
Frosted dreams in silent night,
With giggles that feel just right.

The Warmth of Quiet Companionship

On a couch, two friends do chill,
With popcorn bowls we never fill.
Binge-watching shows until we snore,
Snuggled up, who could ask for more?

Comfort food and silly fights,
Addressing life's weird little plights.
Losing track of every time,
While sipping tea and sharing rhyme.

Our dogs fight over who's the best,
While we just lounge, forget the rest.
In quiet dawn, our hearts feel full,
With friends like these, life's never dull!

A comfy blanket, cozy glow,
Together, we steal the show.
In warmth of friendship, we unite,
Silly giggles feel just right.

Ties Untold in the Silent Night

Under stars, secrets unfold,
Whispers shared, stories told.
In the fog, we tie our shoes,
One size fits, but none to choose!

With every tie, a memory's pressed,
In the dark, we've made our quest.
Shadows dance, the moon's in sight,
Holding hands feels just so right.

Ghosts might dance on chilly grass,
But our laughs, they always last.
With no more questions, just delight,
Ties untold in the silent night.

The playful breeze begins to flow,
As we wander, toe to toe.
With ties unbound, hearts ignite,
Shared laughter glows, pure delight.

Idyllic Moments Among Twinkling Lights

Under strings of twinkling glare,
Each bulb's a thought, we gladly share.
Hot dogs roasted, tales of yore,
While critters cheer and ask for more.

Sipping cider that's way too sweet,
Dancing barefoot with chilly feet.
In the flicker, our worries fade,
As memories sing in joyful parade.

Laughter echoes in the night,
Chasing fireflies, oh what a sight!
Caught while laughing, feeling right,
Idyllic moments, pure and bright.

Adventurous sparks fill the air,
With every giggle, we feel the flare.
Among twinkling lights, hearts take flight,
In those moments, life feels just right.

Dances of Hearts in the Frost

In winter's chill, we twist and twirl,
With frosty breath and hearts in whirl.
Our jackets squeak, our noses red,
We glide like penguins, but it's widespread.

Snowflakes land upon our toes,
You trip and fall, I laugh, it shows.
Your hot cocoa spills, oh what a mess,
It warms my heart, can you confess?

We build a snowman, lumpy and round,
He wears your hat; he looks profound.
We dance around, a humorous sight,
He's got more moves than me tonight!

And as we twirl, the stars peek through,
Our frosty hearts beat loud and true.
With every giggle, the night takes flight,
In frosty dances, love feels just right.

The Exchange of Silent Heartbeats

Across the room, our eyes collide,
Your heart's a drum, and I'm the ride.
No words are said, yet feelings soar,
I smile at you, and you just snore.

We sit in silence, it's quite a scene,
Your sandwich crumbs? Oh, pristine!
I nod and wink, you raise an eyebrow,
I'm having fun, but you don't know how.

The clock ticks loud, it steals our game,
Our silent language can't be tamed.
Your foot's a-tap, my hand's a-wave,
With every heartbeat, we're quite the rave!

But suddenly, your phone does ring,
A heartfelt song? And I can't sing!
I try to dance with my silent soul,
In our stillness, we both feel whole.

Stolen Moments by the Firelight

The flames flicker, shadows play,
We throw marshmallows, hip-hip-hooray!
Your funny faces, I can't resist,
With all this laughter, nothing's amiss.

We roast our dreams like those gooey treats,
Sharing secrets, and silly beats.
The night's a canvas, our laughter paints,
From cheesy jokes to silly faint.

As firelight dances, sparks ignite,
Wrong turns lead to pure delight.
You snort with laughter, I cannot breathe,
In stolen moments, our hearts bequeath.

With each warm sip of cocoa bold,
We share our stories, shyly told.
In the warmth of fire, the world is right,
Together we bask, till the morning light.

Intricate Patterns of Connection

In tangled yarns, our thoughts entwine,
A friendship that's a bit divine.
We knit together, stitch by stitch,
Creating laughter, no need to hitch.

The patterns twist, they sometimes fray,
But through it all, we find our way.
Your puns are weird, but they make me grin,
In this crazy dance, we always win!

With artful strokes, we sketch our days,
In intricate patterns, lively ways.
Our laughter echoes, a joyful sound,
In this crazy world, true friends are found.

So let's keep weaving this tale so grand,
With every stitch, we understand.
In life's great fabric, with love we thread,
In intricate patterns, our hearts are fed.

Echoes of Love in Winter's Breath

In winter's chill, my heart's a freeze,
I love you, darling, but pass the cheese.
Your laughter echoes, though snowflakes fall,
Together we warm, through it all.

Hot cocoa sips, with marshmallows float,
You steal my heart, and half my coat.
Winter nights with blankets tight,
We cuddle and snack, a lovely sight.

But when you snore, it's quite a feat,
Like Santa's sleigh, you stomp the street.
Yet I don't mind, it's all in fun,
At least I know, you're the only one.

So here's to love in frosty days,
To mittens, kisses, and silly ways.
With every snowman we might make,
I promise it's love, not just hot cake.

Hidden Longings Under the Garland

Under the garland, I found a gift,
A box of jokes, to give your heart a lift.
My secret crush, oh what a mess,
Who knew love could cause such distress?

Tangled lights and tangled fate,
You took too long to operate.
Each bulb we plug, sparks joy and dread,
But wrapped in love, we'll forge ahead.

Your holiday sweater, a fashion crime,
It should be banned for all of time.
Yet still I smile with every glance,
For my hidden longing, you leave me in trance.

So let us dance beneath the mistletoe,
With laughter loud, and cheeks aglow.
In this strange season, we'll find our way,
Where hidden longings are here to stay.

Soft Confessions in the Night

As stars peek out, I sneak a sigh,
Your snoring echoes, it makes me cry.
I confess my love in whispers so soft,
But your pillow talks back, and off we scoff.

Candlelight flickers, shadows do sway,
A secret cheer awaits the day.
I try to say, you're my heart's light,
But you just mumble, 'Not now, it's night.'

With each soft laugh, side-splitting glee,
Your face scrunched up, as cute as can be.
Yet beneath the cover of dark, we share,
Our secrets and dreams, no doubts, just care.

So here's to the mischief, the giggles abound,
In soft confessions, love can be found.
With every snicker and every little fight,
Together we shine, soft hearts alight.

Enchanted Whispers of Yuletide

In the glow of the fir, magic is near,
Your dance moves resemble a startled deer.
With tinsel in hand, we twirl and spin,
This Yuletide joy, where do I begin?

Cookies and laughter, an icing dream,
You taste the batter, oh what a scheme!
With flour on noses, and giggles galore,
In our enchanted kitchen, who could ask for more?

Pine-scented wishes, hot chocolate tides,
We dream of snowflakes as fun time slides.
But when you trip on the Christmas lights,
It's a winter wonderland of silly sights.

So let us toast with clinking mugs,
To warm our hearts and share the hugs.
In whispers soft, our love's a blast,
Enchanted moments, forever to last.

Secrets Passed in the Silk of December

In whispers soft, the snowflakes fall,
While cats in boots have a winter brawl.
A squirrel in shades, cool as can be,
Dances on rooftops, wild and free.

Hot cocoa spills, a marshmallow fly,
As kids run by, with a snowman sigh.
Their noses red, like ripe cherries there,
Caught in snowballs, there's chaos everywhere.

The frostbite nibbles at all those toes,
While mom's friends gather, gossip in rows.
A grandpa snorts, wraps his scarf too tight,
And calls it fashion, oh what a sight!

The night's secrets hide in sparkling light,
As stars giggle down, a comical sight.
December's charm with laughter does blend,
While snowmen conspire, their plans to upend.

The Language of Frosty Kisses

With frosty breath, they steal a tease,
The snowflakes wink, as they swirl with ease.
A snowman whispers to the wind so sweet,
While raindrops giggle and tap those feet.

Hot soup on the stove makes a merry sound,
While cats play chase all around the ground.
Frosty kisses on cheeks like a prank,
Invisible hugs, in winter's blank flank.

With snowball fights and some secret codes,
They strategize under old tree roads.
A snow angel waves, with a frosty flair,
While the postman slides past, unaware.

Giggles erupt from a warm, cozy place,
As cocoa spills on the warm, fuzzy lace.
Frosty whispers that tickle the nose,
Turn winter's chill into laughter that grows.

Enigmas Wrapped in Yuletide Green

In the tangle of lights, a mystery brews,
With trees wearing hats made of dazzling hues.
Ornaments giggle on branches above,
While elves trade secrets wrapped tight with love.

Garlands of laughter in every cheer,
As mistletoes plot with a sly little leer.
A partridge croons atop the year's tree,
While grumpy old Santa tries to agree.

Chasing reindeer in pajamas absurd,
Hilarity reigns, oh haven't you heard?
The presents conspire with ribbons so bright,
While peppers and onions dance through the night.

In this puzzling season, all's merry and bright,
As holiday cheer takes a comical flight.
Questions abound, wrapped in green delight,
While laughter ignites in the soft candlelight.

Echoes of Hearts in the Candlelight

In shuttered rooms, the shadows prance,
As awkward couples try to dance.
With flickering flames and a dinner so grand,
They fumble their words, slip out of hand.

Sweethearts blush with a clumsy grin,
As forks go flying, and giggles begin.
The candle gleams on dishes so bright,
While desserts disappear, much to their fright.

Hearts echo softly beneath the glow,
While laughter flows in a romantic show.
A saucy remark breaks the evening quiet,
As love's sweet antics start a small riot.

In the warmth of night, a promise is spun,
With funny quirks, romance weighs a ton.
With candles flickering and warmth in the air,
These echoes entwine in the night, a sweet snare.

A Tapestry of Unshared Dreams

I tried to weave a dream so bright,
But every thread escaped my sight.
A tapestry of hopes so grand,
Yet all I have is a rubber band.

I thought I'd catch the perfect scheme,
Instead, I made a meme of a meme.
My fellow dreamers, oh so sly,
They laughed and said, "Oh me, oh my!"

I tossed my plans like paper kites,
But they got stuck in tree tops' heights.
A funny sight, my dreams took flight,
But fell like leaves on a Halloween night.

Next time I'll keep my goals inside,
Or maybe share them with a guide.
For now, I'll just embrace the tease,
And hope for dreams that come with ease.

Gathering Stars in the Cold Night

I stepped outside to catch a star,
But slipped on ice and fell afar.
With snowflakes dancing on my nose,
I learned the stars have sneaky prose.

I reached up high, with hands outstretched,
But found that every wish was etched.
In ice that crystalized my fate,
I guess that stars just love to skate!

I called to friends, "Let's have some fun!"
But all they brought was puns on puns.
"Let's gather stars," said one aloud,
But tripped and fell, becoming proud.

So here we lie under the sky,
With frozen dreams and snacks piled high.
Next time I'll wear my best warm coat,
And avoid the starry ice cream float!

Furtive Glances Among the Leaves

Beneath the trees, I thought I'd hide,
From that squirrel who dared to chide.
With furtive glances, we exchanged,
A battle of wits, all prearranged.

The wind said, "Shh! Here comes the owl,"
Who flew right by with a hungry howl.
The squirrel chattered, "What's your game?"
I threw a seed — it fell with shame.

The leaves around began to laugh,
As my dignity split in half.
For creatures tiny and large alike,
Were picking on my social bike.

Next time I'll wear a clever mask,
And avoid this woodland task.
For furtive glances can reveal,
That sometimes, pride's a spinning wheel!

Echoing in the Stillness of Winter

Winter whispers through the night,
With frosty breath and stars so bright.
But when I called, "Hey, how do you do?"
An echo laughed, "I'm not talking to you!"

I followed it outside my door,
And slipped right on the cold, hard floor.
"Snow, you joker!" I let out a shout,
As flakes kept falling all about.

An echo's jest is never kind,
It lingers long, a hard rewind.
It gives me laughs, my face turns red,
But silent nights fill me with dread.

So here I stand in winter's glare,
With echoes rumbling everywhere.
Next time I'll look and think it through,
For winter's jokes are often true!

Hushed Wishes in Evergreen

Underneath the spruce so tall,
Whispers bounce off walls of green.
Squirrels plotting, never small,
Dreams of nuts, their daily scene.

Robins gossip, chirp and sing,
About that nut that got away.
The trees, they sway, a graceful swing,
As nature laughs at yesterday.

A raccoon drones on with flair,
"Who stole my snacks? I'm sure of this!"
While owls hoot, a knowing stare,
"Just take a nap, you'll never miss!"

Wishes cling to every pine,
Like ornaments for a joke,
The woodland's humor, pure divine,
In chuckles shared, the magic's woke.

Conspiracies of the Night Chill

In shadows deep, the cats convene,
Plotting dreams of midnight theft.
While mice in corners, sleek and keen,
Whisper, 'We'll leave them bereft.'

Owl keeps watch with a knowing grin,
A sentinel of tricks in play.
The moonlight casts a magic spin,
As laughter echoes, night's ballet.

Ghosts of secrets flutter by,
"Did you hear about that lost shoe?"
Skipping whispers, oh so spry,
Legends grow with each ado!

But as dawn breaks, conspiracies fade,
The cats retreat to warming nooks,
While mice rejoice in the charade,
Pleased with their nightly plucky hooks.

Subtle Murmurs in the Snow

Snowflakes dance like giggling sprites,
Covering the world in white.
Bunnies bounce in pure delight,
Crafting tunnels, what a sight!

Cardinals squabble, bright and bold,
Over seeds stashed deep below.
"Mine!" cries one, "Don't be so cold!"
While squirrels scold, "Hey, take it slow!"

The wind whispers, tales of old,
Of snowmen with their silly hats.
A carrot nose, a sight to behold,
In winter's play, everyone chats.

As winter wears her frosty crown,
Laughter fills the crisp, clear air.
Each flake falls with a gentle frown,
The secrets of snow declare.

Gentle Secrets in the Air

Breezes carry laughter near,
Where daisies weave their tales so sweet.
A bumblebee with charm sincere,
Mixes nectar, oh what a treat!

Clouds drift by with dreamy lore,
Sharing jokes in whispered tones.
The sun peeks through, it starts to roar,
As flowers giggle, "Look, we're grown!"

A butterfly plans a fancy flight,
"Tomorrow's party, dress to impress!"
While ladybugs gather in delight,
Their polka dots a bold success!

As day slips into twilight's glow,
The air hums with tales anew.
Gentle secrets start to flow,
In nature's play, we find our cue.

Radiance of Unseen Devotion

In a world where socks go missing,
My love for you is out of sight.
Like that slice of cake you're wishing,
I'll find it in the fridge tonight.

When you steal the covers at dawn,
I giggle, though you don't awake.
Our love's a silent, sleepy brawn,
Wrapped up in warmth like a cake.

Your jokes may land like lead balloons,
But still, they make my heart do flips.
In the quiet hum of afternoon,
Our laughter spills like cheesy quips.

So here's a toast, let's raise a cup,
To love that's bright but slightly bent.
In all its quirks, we still hold up,
Radiance in every single dent.

The Magic of Hidden Touches

A tickle fight right by the sink,
Who knew that dish soap's so much fun?
Those fingerprints in ketchup ink,
A culinary treasure hunt begun.

Your warm embrace, a great disguise,
That nearly turns me into goo.
While you steal fries and roll your eyes,
It's moments like this I love you too.

The dance we do while out to shop,
It's not the groceries, it's the sway.
Your clumsy moves make my heart hop,
In random aisles, we find our play.

So let's embrace this wacky ride,
With magic found in every touch.
In hidden quirks, my heart's your guide,
For simple love means so much.

Tenderness Drifting on the Chill

When winter winds begin to howl,
You steal my chocolate — oh, how rude!
But in your laugh, I can't help growl,
For sweetness, it's not just the food.

We sit by fires, your gaze aflame,
Cozy warmth wrapped like a burrito.
Your frozen feet deserve some blame,
Yet love's the best heating, don't you know?

Snowflakes swirl like whispers soft,
As we build snowmen with old coats.
While my nose runs, I'm still held aloft,
In love's warm scarf, we share our hopes.

So let it chill; we'll knit a scarf,
One stitch at a time, side by side.
In winter's grip, we find our half,
Tenderness grows, we cannot hide.

Secrets Laced with Snowflakes

In the quiet of a snowy day,
I found your stash of hidden snacks.
Those cookies, dear, they led me astray,
Now I must cover my tracks.

Each snowflake holds a whispered thought,
Like you and me playing hide and seek.
Your secret giggles I have caught,
In the frost, our love's unique peak.

With cocoa mugs, we tell tall tales,
Of snowmen with questionable hats.
And while the winter blizzard wails,
We huddle close with our silly chats.

So here's to secrets, icy and sweet,
Hidden treasures we both adore.
In every flake, our laughter meets,
As snowflakes drift, love's evermore.

Milton Keynes UK
Ingram Content Group UK Ltd.
UKHW020345031224
452051UK00007B/174